EQUINE DO

The Way of the Horse

DINO FRETTERD

ARPress

ILLUMINATING IDEAS.
EMPOWERING VOICES

ARPress LLC
45 Dan Road Suite 5
Canton MA 02021
Hotline: 1(888) 821-0229
Fax: 1(508) 545-7580

Ordering Information:
Quantity sales. Special discounts are available on quantity purchases by corporations, associations, and others. For details, contact the publisher at the address above.

Printed in the United States of America.

ISBN-13:   Softcover   979-8-89356-666-6
            eBook   979-8-89356-667-3

Library of Congress Control Number: 2024903600

CONTENTS

Every decade or so, someone in the horse industry comes along and defines a new way of looking at an old subject. Dino is just that person. He has managed to see the horse in a different light and actually use the science of biomechanics to show the form and function of the horse from it's head to it's toe. Dino started out working with humans in the field of musculoskeletal manipulation. He simply switched over to horses due to a profound love of this beautiful animal.

Dino observes the form and function of the horse while they are standing still and when they are moving. He has taken these techniques to a new level—GENIUS!!! Dino taught himself all there is to know about the horse's teeth, muscles and feet and studied how they interact with each other in performance situations or in trail riding. In this book, Dino explains in detail, new concepts which have not previously been defined by anyone else! He has included illustrations along with text that can give the equine professional and the average lay horse owner a chance to understand how their horse works. I believe you will find his writing both enjoyable and enlightening.

James A. Giacopuzzi, DVM/Farrier

The Story Of Roxanne

Roxanne is our 17-year-old Palomino. My wife and I got both her and her Mother Candy when she was 5 years old. She and Candy lived on a 10-acre pasture with little human contact. Roxanne only had her feet trimmed once in all that time she would not let anyone get near her. It took 2 weeks at our farm to be able to touch her.

I began working with her and in a few weeks we were riding. She seemed to be happy with her new life. At this time my work took me away from home a lot and Roxanne got left behind again. We had 7 horses at the time 5 mares and 2 stallions and Roxanne was low mare in the pecking order. She was constantly being pushed around and was always on guard. Over time she had become so tensed in both mind and body that she didn't want to be touched because it hurt. I didn't make this connection until I met Dino.

I thought she needed to go back to school thinking she had forgotten her training with a little work her attitude had gotten better but still guarded. It was only when I had Dino come to my farm that I learned the truth about Roxanne (as it turned out I learned a lot more about horses and their behavior through Dino). She was in knots and her own body was her enemy human touch was painful.

When Dino first met Roxanne, he pointed out all of her problem areas and immediately went to work on them. Of course Roxanne saw him as the enemy and would rather have bitten his head off instead of having to endure his touch. You could see the change come over Roxanne as Dino continued to work on her. Her whole body began to soften, of course there was the tell tale licking of the lips we all know about but you could see the changes in her face the snarl went away and she had bedroom eyes. It was a complete 180-degree in her demeanor. By the end of the session Roxanne was showing Dino her gratitude she didn't want him to stop the session she was feeling that great, Dino taught my wife and I what we needed do to continue to help resolve Roxanne's body issues.

Today thanks to Dino Roxanne is a much happier horse.

Anthony Madaia, Barefoot Equine Podiatrist

Equine—Do

"THE WAY OF THE HORSE"

Introduction

A guidebook teaching you to:

"**Look**" at "**See**" and "**Understand**" your horse

Sharing information is invaluable, sharing knowledge is empowering. Knowledge is not attained through reading and memorizing, but through understanding and application. A great author said "To be successful, you must have a definite purpose."

The definite purpose of this book is to share information and knowledge (based on facts and not opinion) with all those who love horses and want to understand not only how to see postural faults that compromise comfort and performance, but also have a desire to make the necessary changes to better them. I will reference some of the common problems you may be experiencing with your horse therefore allowing you to have a better understanding of where the issues may be coming from. A better understanding is a more educated horse owner, and a more educated horse owner saves money.

Better posture equals better performance.

All too often horses are described as having conformational issues when in many cases; they merely have an imbalance in posture. This manual will help get beyond 'conformation' to having a much clearer understanding of how to LOOK, SEE and UNDERSTAND the horse in a whole new way.

With over 30 years of bodywork experience, I feel it is time to share what I have learned with those who are seeking a true solution. Everything here has a purpose, and I will refer to the following Concepts and Components as fact, not opinion. In other words, I am not the one who came up with how things work . . . I simply apply the rules. I can HONESTLY say that each person with whom I have shared this understanding with have responded the same way by saying "that just makes sense".

If you take the necessary time and be patient you will see results. The exercises, which will be described to you, with the accompanying photos, will give you a very clear understanding of how to properly perform these exercises. Remember . . . no one goes to the gym and exercises one day and then looks in the mirror and says, "wow . . . look at me!" But with proper technique and practice, you will see changes not only in posture and performance, but also in your relationship with your horse.

This is <u>not</u> intended to diagnose but to evaluate and assess. If you are having a serious problem with your horse you should seek veterinary care.

Chapter 1

Concepts and Components

This manual will help you understand the application of three Concepts and three Components.

The Three Concepts (or natural laws):

- <u>Function:</u> to operate normally, fulfilling a purpose or role (as defined in a dictionary) will be discussed with respect to the three components listed below

- <u>Balance:</u> the point of equilibrium (no greater stress in any one direction)

- <u>Gravity:</u> the force that draws everything downward toward the ground (earth)

The Three Components:

- <u>The Teeth and TMJ (jaw)</u>

- <u>The Body; musculoskeletal structure</u>

- <u>The Feet; hooves or foundation</u>

All of the components tie together: limitation of function creates imbalances and neuromuscular compensations. This creates postural faults in the horse and then you are dealing with nature's force of gravity acting on these faults.

An imbalance in any one of the above listed components has a direct affect on another. You will learn how to apply simple visual and practical assessments to determine the state of balance in your horse.

Although this is not a manual which teaches bodywork, I will explain a few "easy to perform" techniques to help and/or check for some imbalances. Included are several photos from clinics in which the horse owners are applying the techniques and information I have shared with them to help transform their horse. I describe "how", as well as "where" and "why". For those interested in learning more, clinics and the "Equine~Do Institute" classes are available.

I will use various analogies in this to give you an entertaining and simple way to understand how something may function for different parts of the horse such as: The Bear Cave, The Master Link, The Transmission, The Park Bench, and The Boom of a Crane, Water Balloons, Dinner Plate, The Speed Boat and The Anchor.

I will use terms such as checking the Dinner Plate, Giving Peace, Jaws of Life, and Going to the Gas Station.

I will start by applying the concepts (which are based in natural laws) to the components described above to provide you with an easy to understand format. So, let's start with:

Applying the concept of Function of the teeth and TMJ

The function of the teeth is obvious . . . it's what horses chew with. So let's break this down by starting with the incisors. The first and foremost job of the incisors is to rip and tear grass. Unfortunately for most domesticated horses this is taken out of the equation. They are fed processed hay in which they are using their lips to bring the hay into their mouths. This takes away the natural function of abrading or wear. Ever hear the term "long in the tooth?" This refers to an older domesticated horse that has not had proper dental care. You will not find a wild horse that is long in the tooth because they naturally forage. You should know that when the horse chews from side to side, the incisors play a crucial role in translation or movement. Excessive length of the incisors also plays an important role in inhibiting the anterior/posterior/bilateral movements of the temporomandibular joint.

The back teeth (molars) are where the chewing really happens. If the horse has ATR (accentuated transverse ridges), ramps or hyper eruption in the molar arcade you will again see a limitation in the anterior and/or posterior (forward and backward) as well as bilateral (side to side) movements of the jaw caused by these obstacles.

Applying the concept of Balance of the teeth and TMJ

The spacing of the temporomandibular joint should be equal on both sides. If the horse has the same teeth on both sides, and they are in balance, it makes sense that the spacing should be equal? The temporomandibular joint is the joint that allows the horse to open and close the mouth as well allowing anterior/posterior and bilateral (forward, backward and side to side) movement.

(Proper hand placement to assess TMJ)

(Alternate hand placement for assessing the TMJ spacing)

(Identifying TMJ)

All these movements functioning properly allow the horse to maintain a relaxed head and neck posture. Dysfunction of one of these natural movements will compromise the horse in motion as well as in static or standing position.

Applying the concept of Gravity to the teeth and TMJ

If a horse has a malocclusion (undesirable positioning of teeth), it will cause discomfort in the mouth, thus forcing the horse to find what might be called a convenience bite. The horse will find a place that lessens the discomfort by contracting muscles on one side to avoid the discomfort. This also creates a shift in the TMJ, or compression to one side. Since the mandible of the horse has weight and that weight is shifted due to neuromuscular contraction, it obviously changes the balance of the bone itself. This is where gravity takes over.

Applying the concept of Function to the musculoskeletal structure

Muscles function in a three-phase cycle: excitation, contraction and relaxation. To put this in simpler terms think of it like this; the **excitation** is the thought translating into a chemical release going to the muscle thus creating a firing of the muscle fiber or **contraction** of the muscle. It follows that, if you want continued movement, with the muscle relaxing so the process can be repeated.

Applying the concept of Balance to the musculoskeletal structure

Balance of the musculoskeletal structure means each muscle and joint of the body is capable of performing throughout a full range of motion. If there is tension or tightness in a muscle/ group, there is an imbalance of the musculoskeletal structure due to the contraction of one muscle and the elongation of the opposite muscle. This then obviously puts stress to the skeletal structure (joints) to which the muscles are attached.

All muscles have an opposing force or action. So when one muscle or group of muscles contract, their opposite muscle or group must be relaxed to allow full range of motion to take place. Just like a pulley system, one side pulls as the others side gives. To better understand muscle imbalance, I would like you to imagine a game of tug of war where you have five people on one side and four on the other. When the five people collectively pull they have a force generated in that direction, but when the four people pull on their side, they cannot pull equally. When a muscle(s) is in a continually contracted state it makes it more difficult for the opposite side to perform properly.

Applying the concept of Gravity to the musculoskeletal structure

Simply put, if muscles are imbalanced due to stress and one muscle or group of muscles are in a contracted state, the opposite muscles are being stretched. Think of leaning forward. You get to a point where you can hold your balance by constricting your toes so you don't fall. As long as you hold yourself in this state you won't fall, but as soon as you stop the contraction . . . gravity pulls you forward.

Applying the concept of Function to the hoof

The hoof of the horse has different functions so I will describe each one so you have a clear understanding:

The first function is to provide support; it's what they stand on. The next function is to create flight (or direction) of the appendage. We are all aware of the fact that you walk differently in different shoes.

If someone were to glue a pop sickle stick to your shoe on one side or the other, this would totally change how your foot leaves the ground. After the hoof leaves the ground it must land. So think again of the pop sickle stick under your shoe and how you would land on your foot. This is an important factor with respect to the dissipation of concussive forces. If you leave the ground awkwardly you will land the same way. One clear sign of this imbalance would be a horse that has splints. The excessive concussion to one side of the hoof creates trauma to the leg, particularly the cannon bone, and the (interosseous) ligament that connects the splint bones. Constant trauma to this area tells the body to repair the damage by lying down calcium . . . hence you have a splint.

As the hoof lands on the ground we now have compression of the digital cushion or bulbous tissue, which acts as a pump assisting the lymphatic and venous blood flow to travel back up the leg. Think of a stocked up horse. One factor in stocking up may simply be the lack of function of this process in the digital cushion.

Applying the concept of Balance to the hoof

Balance of the hoof means there is no greater stress in any one direction in its distribution of weight. You often see imbalances of the hoof through the high heel/low heel syndrome. Balance of the foot means all parts of the hoof get an equal blood supply. Hoof growth is based on blood flow and blood flow is dictated by pressure. Blood flowing from an area of high-pressure speeds growth of that less pressured part of the hoof.

Applying the concept of Gravity to the hoof

Gravity is the force that draws everything downward toward the ground, and since the hoof is the contact point to the ground. It will grow purely based on the balance of the three components. "Gravity always takes its toll".

The following analogies will give you a different perspective of the feet (hooves) as well as the TMJ (temporomandibular joint) and the body (musculoskeletal structure) as well as some assessment techniques that are easy to follow and apply.

Chapter 2

ANALOGIES

The Million-dollar check analogy

Think of this analogy . . . someone hands you a check for one million dollars and tells you that it is yours to keep and cash, with one little catch; if you can hold it for one month without letting it go, it's yours. How much pressure does it require for you to hold a piece of paper? Not much right? But are you willing to let go of your financial stability? Well let's translate this into muscle function. The muscles you are using to hold that check stay in a contracted state while the opposite muscle stays in an elongated state. So think of how much harder it is for the opposing group to perform. Remember the "tug of war" analogy; there is always more pull from one side than the other. If I try to pry your fingers from that check your instant reaction is to contract your fingers in order to secure your stability. This is a good way to understand how much harder one muscle can work against the other. The horse will do the same thing to maintain its postural stability.

The Toll Keepers analogy

You must first understand the weight distribution of a horse's body. All equine anatomy books that I have read state that a horse bears approximately 60% of its weight on the front feet. This is because of the gravity and weight of the head and neck, which are extended in front of the horse. Thus it is obvious that higher the headset, the more the transfer of weight goes caudally or toward the rear of the horse. Now think of a horse "who never grows any heel". We have all heard the saying that "gravity always takes its toll". A hoof is encompassed fluid and has an expansive and contractive phase when landing and leaving the ground. When in a static position, the blood flow travels away from pressure. Therefore if a horse holds their head higher or lower than what provides balance to the hoof, you create a different shape of hoof simply because of uneven weight distribution.

Water Balloons analogy

Another way to think about this is to think of a hoof as a water balloon. The water balloon represents the fluid encompassed hoof. And if you put more pressure in any one direction, the fluid travels to the opposite direction. Hoof growth is created by blood flow. So if there is more pressure to a hoof in any part the blood is forced to the opposite side, hence more growth to the least pressure. If a horse has the high head carriage you will generally see low heels. If a horse has an imbalance on one side (jaw) the horse will brace itself and you will see a larger front foot on one side versus the other. Remember if a horse carries their weight evenly you should have two front feet that look the same . . . . makes sense doesn't it?

Create the shape of foot analogy

This is a great way to understand the hoof and its growth. If you place your palm upward (simulating the ground) and then take a finger (simulating the hoof) and press directly downward you can recreate the shape you are looking at. For instance to simulate a low heeled horse, press the pad of your finger more downward and you will see the cuticle area (the back of your fingernail) will turn white and the tip of your finger will get all of the blood, (you can see this because your fingernail is transparent). Now, to create a clubfoot type horse, press your fingertip directly into your hand and watch the blood go toward the back of your fingernail. This same concept applies laterally for flares, those concave and convex shapes. This also gives you a better understanding of joint pressure and the range of the joint motion. Shape of the foot dictates the flight of appendage.

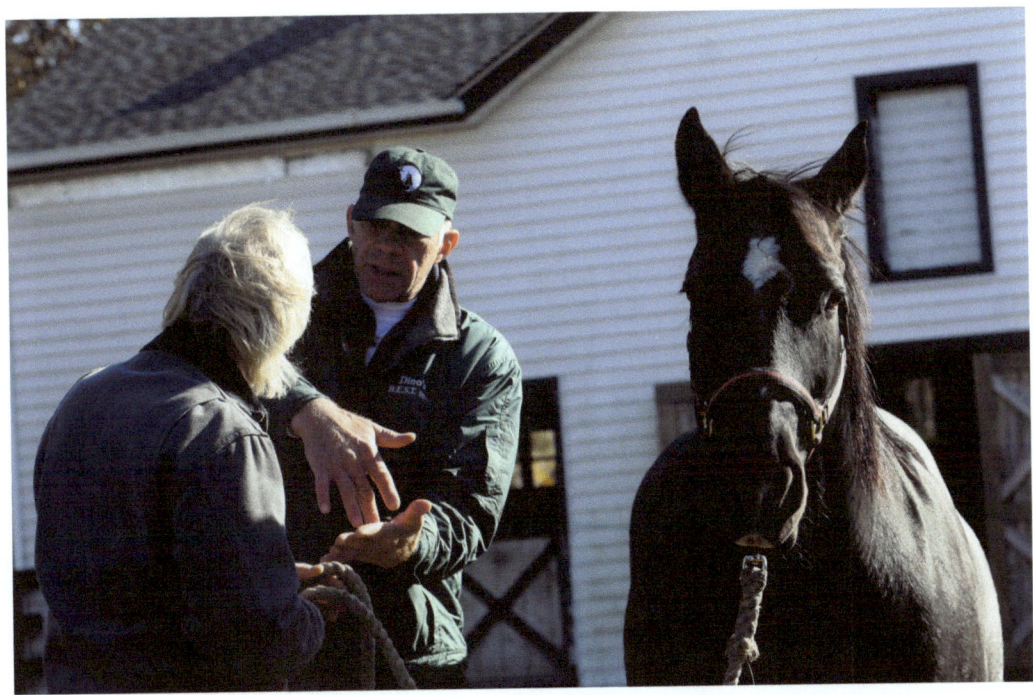

(Recreating shape of hoof)

Riding a motorcycle analogy

To make a motorcycle move you must pull back on the throttle. To perform this action you have to contract the extensor muscles of your forearm, thus pulling (flexing) your wrist backward toward you.

Think of a horse with low heels. He is more than likely stuck in an extended position (as if they were constantly pulling on the throttle) putting excessive stresses (or stretching) to the digital flexor tendons and suspensory ligaments. This does not allow for a fetlock to flex completely backward, which provides full range of motion. This will be further addressed with the Dinner Plate assessment.

We should also talk about the horse that has an upright foot, or in some cases what is called a clubfoot. You may see that this horse is close to, if not over at the knee. The opposite muscles are generally in play here. The flexor muscles of the forelimb are tight disallowing full extension of the hoof. Think of doing this simple test. Make a fist and place it flat on a table with your arm straight. Now lean forward with your weight and you will see your wrist will bend forward. The muscles on the bottom of your forearm will contract and the muscles on the top of your forearm will lengthen causing you to flex your wrist. The carpus or wrist of the horse is commonly referred to as the knee. In either case you have a less than desirable length of stride. By the way, I can't begin to tell you how many times a client has said to me their horse had a "club foot" and after balancing the muscles and mobilizing the joints, to their amazement, the shape of foot had changed. Accompany this with a hoof care provider's accurate trim and you will allow for a much happier hoof and horse. So now you can begin to understand how everything has an effect on something else.

Chapter 3

VISUAL AND ASSESSMENTS

Performing visuals and assessments are easier than you think

So let's start from the bottom and work our way up and through the horse's body. The first thing you can learn to **see** is:

Checking the distance form hairline to the sesamoid bones visual assessment

To see how balanced the horses pastern is, you should look at the distance from the hairline to the small protruding sesamoids bones on the medial (inside) and lateral (outside). Are the distances the same? Do you see a rise in the hairline on the upper edges of the hoof?

(Hairline)

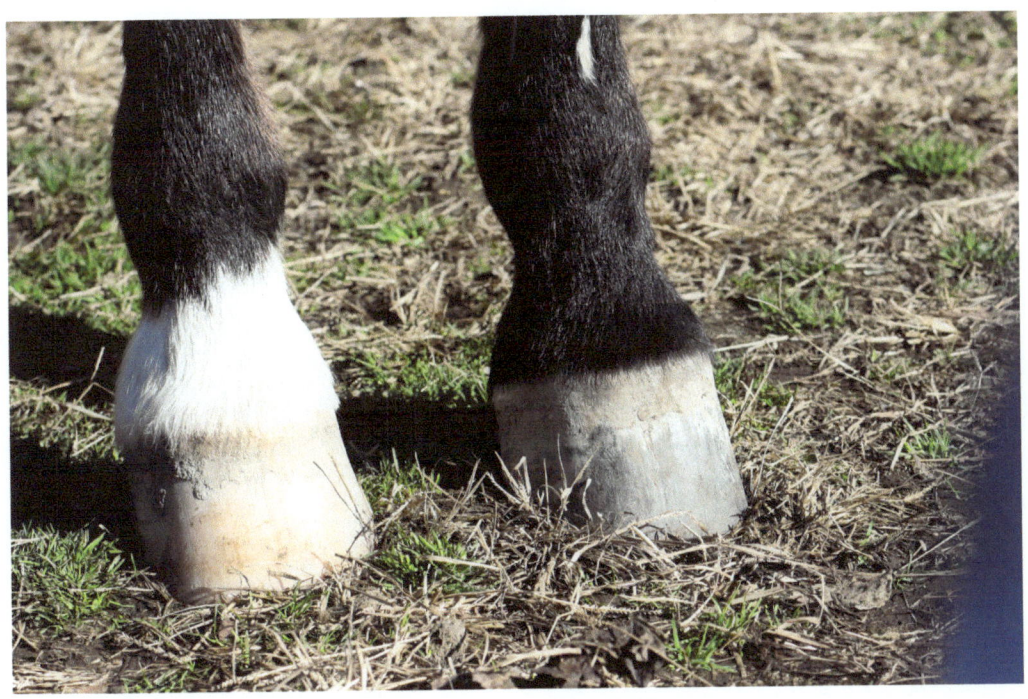

Hairline to Sesamoids

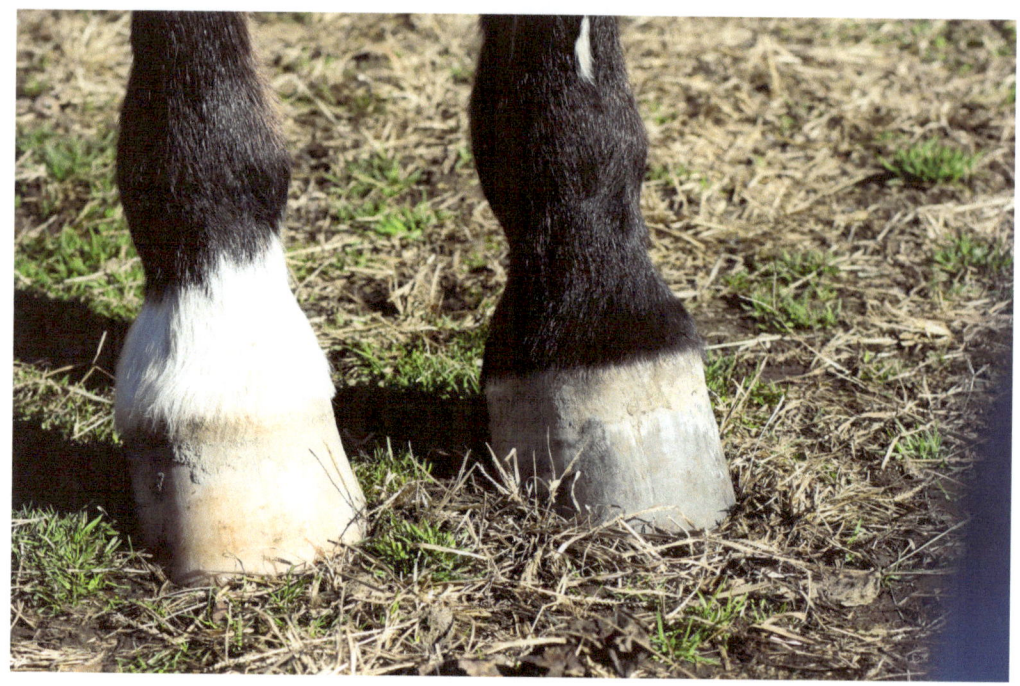

(Distance from hairline to sesamoid)

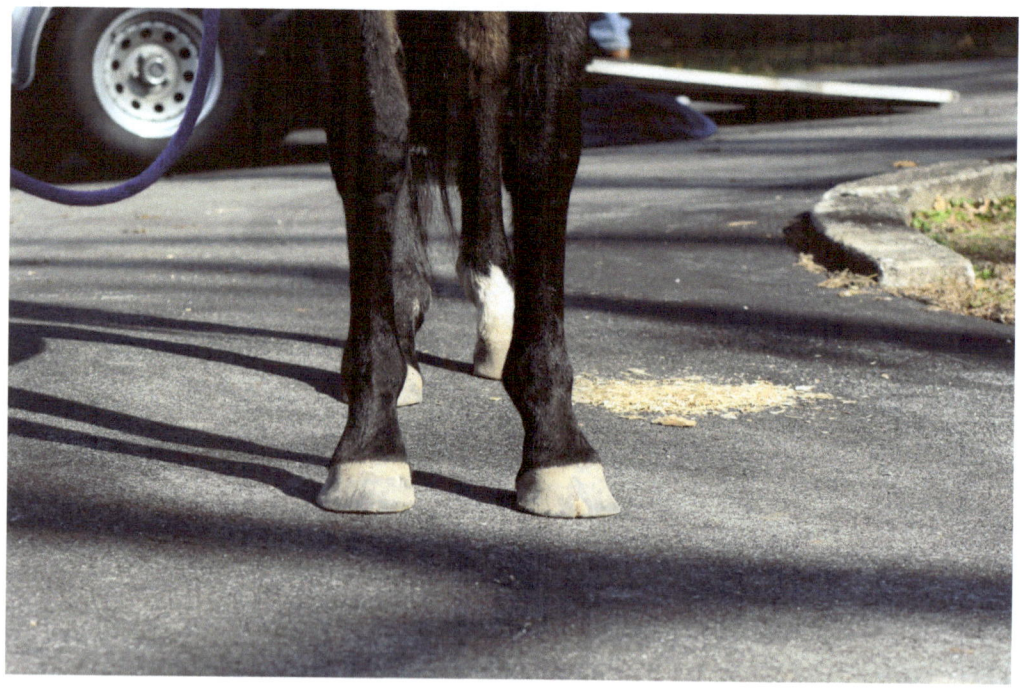

Hairline

Hairline to Sesamoids

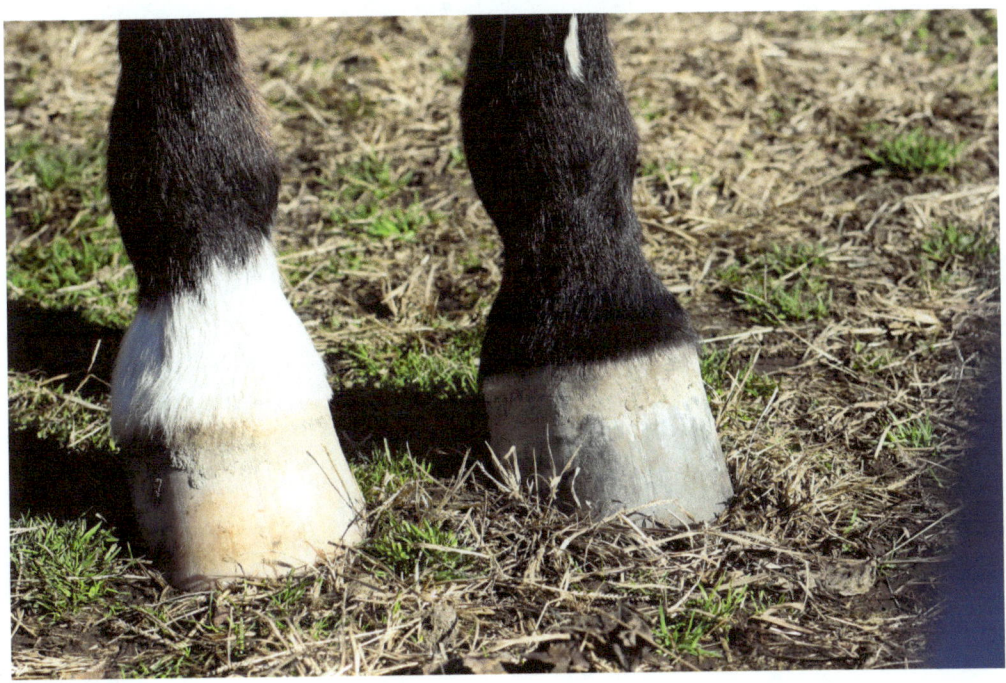

Sesamoids Shock absorbers analogy

I like to refer the sesamoid bones the shock absorbers. The reason for this is that the sesamoid bones are actually part of the suspensory ligaments. When you have restriction of the sesamoids you have excessive concussion to the hoof. Excessive concussion on one side will cause splints. There is a way to assess and restore the mobility of the sesamoids, but although this assessment is not difficult to perform, I feel this is too difficult to explain in this book due to hand position and range of the movement you are looking for. However, I plan to create video clips demonstrating individual techniques.

Checking the Dinner Plate analogy & assessment

I will now refer to the bottom of the hoof as a dinner plate. With this image in mind; think of picking up the foot of your horse to pick out the hoof. You lift it and flex it backward to clean it. Now think of a dinner plate as you flex the foot backward to clean it out and ask yourself . . . . if this was my dinner plate, how much would I get to eat? In other words when you flex the hoof backward to clean it, does the bottom of the hoof become level or does it resist flexing backward comfortably—as flat as a plate? If the hoof does not flex backward comfortably for the horse this means your horse's hoof is not eating a full plate of dirt with every stride. This will create a faster/shorter stride in the horse in that leg. Make sense?

(Flat as a dinner plate)

(Imagine this as a dinner plate)

Dinner Plate

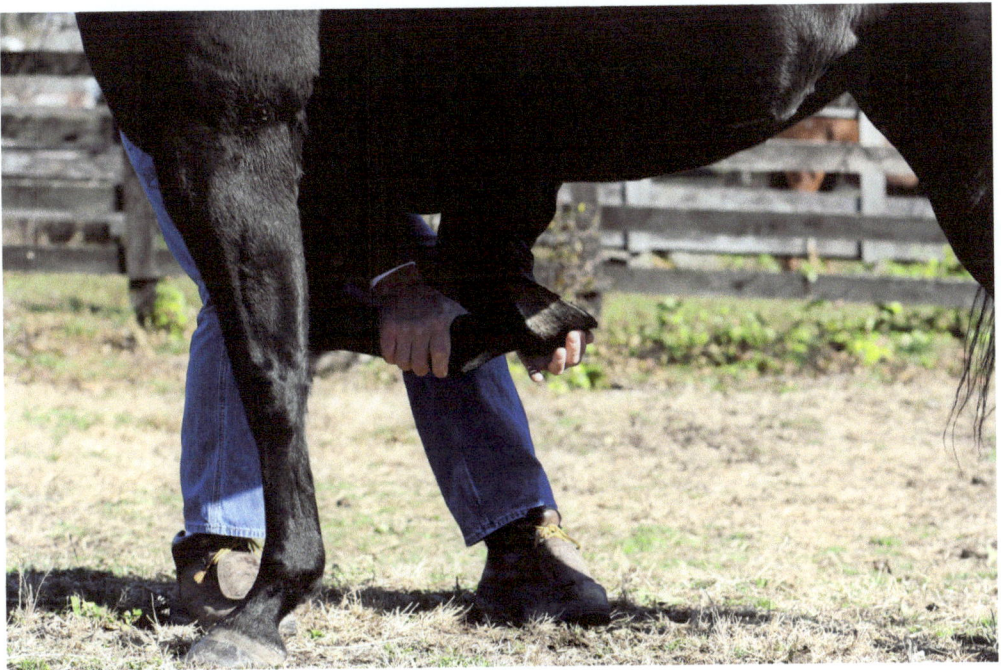

(Proper hard placement is imperative)

What may be causing the lack of motion? If the muscles, which extend the forelimb, are tight (remember riding the motorcycle) the range of motion will be limited in flexion of the hoof. If you observe the photos for checking the dinner plate, you will see how to properly hold the foot and the direction you should gently stretch the hoof to restore full range or a full plate.

The Bear Cave (the mouth) analogy

The reason I like to call the horse's mouth a bear cave is because most people are not willing to venture into something that may have consequences, the horse's mouth anymore than a bear's cave. In other word not many people are willing to stick their hand inside the mouth of a horse to determine if it is having dental issues.

If you were walking through the woods and came across a cave and you knew there were bears in the area, would you go marching in? Or would you look around the outside of the cave for signs that there may be a bear present, like bear droppings, or tracks leading in or out? Do you hear anything from the opening or do you smell anything? There are a number of outward signs telling you there may be something nasty on the inside before you go marching on in.

If a horse has malocclusion (undesirable positioning) of the teeth, this will create abnormal movement of the jaw due to neuromuscular compensation as well as muscle imbalance and periodontal issues. Assessing for signs of something bad on the inside is not difficult at all . . . .

A sign a bear may be present visual/manual assessment

The first thing to look at is the development of the temporal muscles, which are located on the fore head. Simply lift the forelock and ask yourself if they are the same on both sides, or is one larger than the other.

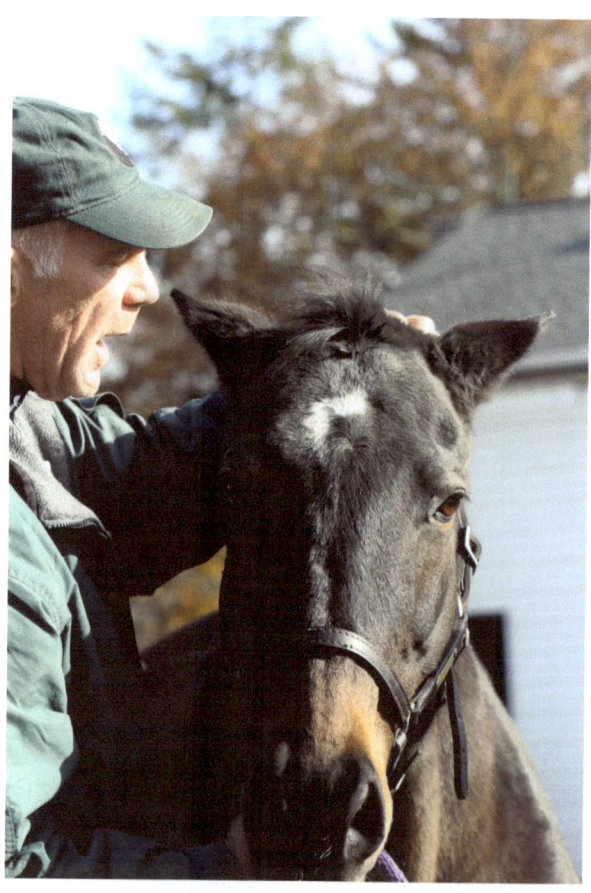

(Looking at and feeling the temporalis muscles size and shape)

Now feel the masseter muscles or (cheek muscles) for the same. Again does one feel larger than the opposite side? These are two major muscles of mastication (chewing) and one larger than the other simply tells you your horse uses the larger side to chew more than the other side. You will notice that if there is over development in one of the temporalis muscles you will also have more muscle mass to the cheek muscle on the same side. This is one indication your horse may have dental issues. Another indication would be your horse favoring the opposite lead of the side

(Feeling for size of masseter muscle)

of over development. For example, if you see a larger temporalis muscle on the right side you will more than likely feel a weakness in the hind left leg of the horse.

The Master Link (TMJ) analogy/ assessment

(Proper hand placement to assess the TMJ and identifying the TMJ space)

Next you can check the space of the temporomandibular joint (TMJ). I like to refer to the TMJ as the master link of the chain on a bicycle. When we were kids and our bike chain broke, we took the bike to be repaired thinking that we needed a new chain. But by simply adding a master link, which holds the chain together, the chain can again function properly in smooth motion. This is the most important joint, allowing the horse freedom of movement throughout the rest of the body. If a horse has a malocclusion (undesirable positioning of teeth) it will cause a restriction of the natural anterior/posterior or forward and backward movement of the jaw. What you will notice is a change or restriction in the neck as well as a degradation of performance.

The first thing you can learn to do is to feel the spacing on both sides of the head at the same time by placing your index finger between the space of the jaw and the temporal bone. I perform this by placing the horse's head on my shoulder while facing the horse. In this position you can take your index finger and place it in between the jaw and the temporal bone with your pinky facing downward and your thumb facing upward. What you are trying to determine is if the space on both sides equal! Is there more space on one side versus the other? Less space on one side will be accompanied by other signs (listed above) that you can physically and visually inspect. You will see that the side with the over developed muscles will have less space in the TMJ on that side.

The Park Bench (balance) analogy/ assessment

If you were sitting on a bench and someone came along and starting lifting one side, naturally you would slide to the opposite direction due to weight and gravity. To keep from sliding, you would either shift your weight toward the person, or brace yourself with your opposite hand. This is called stabilizing. Now let's think of the horse with malocclusion in their mouth (which causes abnormal positioning of the **TMJ**). The mandible has weight to it and if the horses' teeth are out of balance then the jaw is also, and this leads to an attempt to stabilize that imbalance through neuromuscular compensation or bracing. The side that has more compression (less space) is the bracing side and more likely than not the direction of travel the horse prefers least. Another sign to look for an asymmetry is your horse's front feet. An imbalance in the TMJ will cause your horse to load to the opposite side from the bracing and you will see that your horse has one front foot that is larger than the other. Again think of water balloons.

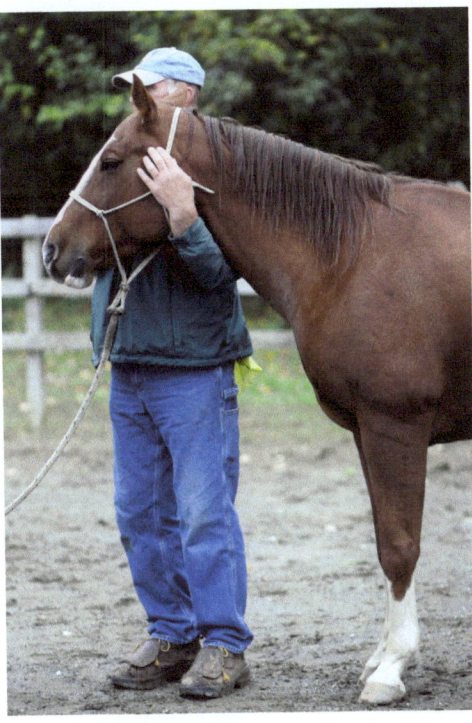

Be sure to check both sides at the same time

Checking the transmission or the anterior/posterior movement of the_TMJ **analogy/ visual/ assessment**

I like to call this a transmission because if you drive an automatic car you can move your gearshift from neutral to drive and neutral to reverse. Being in neutral is in the middle, so if you want to go in reverse you push upward on the handle, and if you want to go into drive you pull downward on the handle. Think of the horses TMJ as the gearshift.

Look at your horse's teeth while he is standing in his normal posture (neutral) and determine where your horse's teeth align. (Upper and lower incisors) Separating the lips does this.

Checking from neutral

While separating the lips, look at your horses teeth to make sure there is contact between the incisors and that there are no obvious spaces at those contact points or any hooks. Also look to see if the teeth line up correctly on each side, and see if one side is inside and the other outside the upper teeth.

(Note the hook on the incisor)

Please note that not all horses' teeth will line up perfectly, but this is not what we are checking for. We are looking for movement forward and backward from wherever our starting point is. Most horses have about 3/8 of an inch of anterior/posterior movement. So this is what you are looking for . . . movement and balance.

When you raise the horse's head there is a natural posterior or backward movement of the teeth and jaw. And when you horse lowers its head (such as while foraging) there is a natural anterior or forward movement.

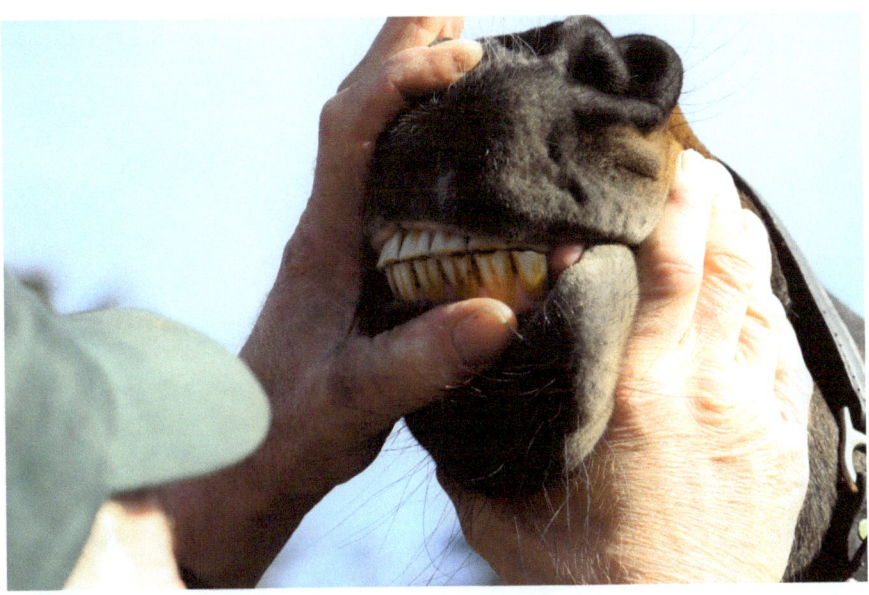

(Checking for posterior movement of the lower jaw)

By the way, our human mouth operates the same way, which you can easily understand by performing this movement. Make contact with your teeth and raise your head upward as if looking at a tall building. You will notice that your lower jaw will slide backward and if you look at your feet with the same contact you will notice that your lower jaw slides forward.

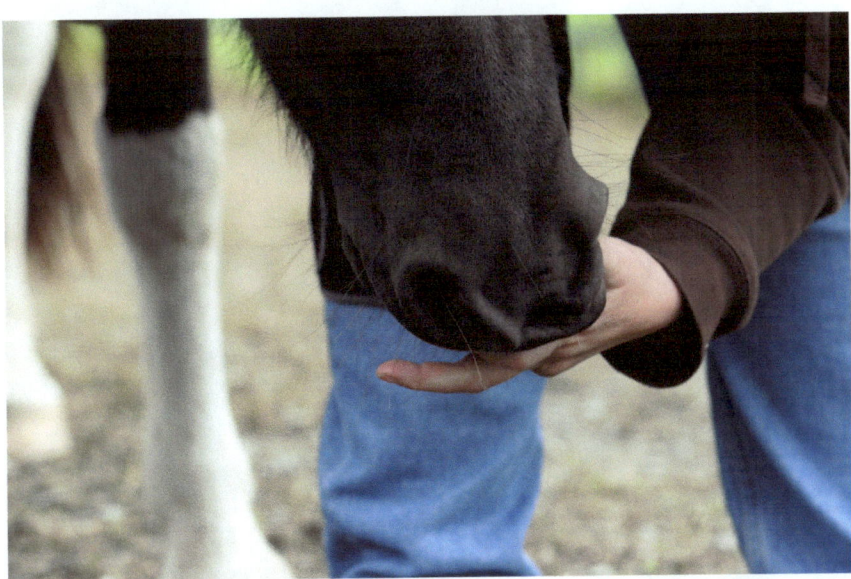

(Checking for anterior movement, lower incisors should move forward)

Checking the jaw/atlas spacing assessment

When checking the spacing between the jaw and atlas (first cervical vertebrae) first make sure the head is straight, then place two fingers (index and middle finger) facing upward between the space of the jaw and first cervical vertebrae (wing of the atlas) and ask yourself if the spacing is the same. This will tell you if your horse's jaw is posterior (backward) and/or if the first cervical is misaligned. Your fingers are the same on both sides, so you should feel equal spacing if the jaw and atlas are in proper position. If not, I suggest you contact your equine dentist or chiropractor to do any further assessment. Remember, you already have the tools to check for signs of a bear.

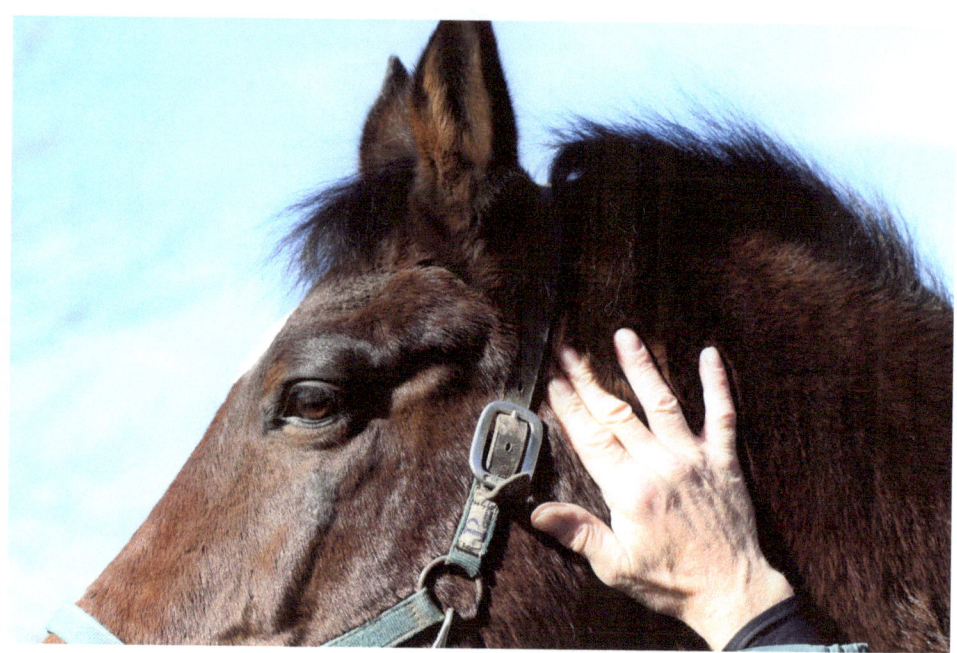

(Proper hand placement)

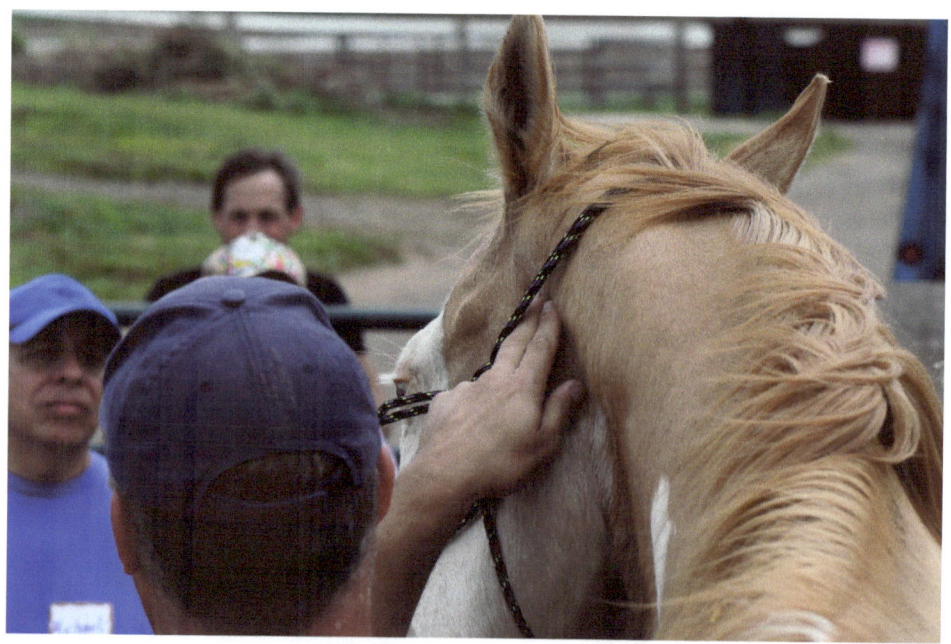

(Identifying Jaw/Atlas spacing)

When looking at the head and neck of the horse, just think of:

The Boom of a Crane analogy/ visual assessment

When looking at the head and neck of the horse, just think of the boom of a crane. I am referring to the horse's head and neck with this analogy because it raises and lowers just the same. To better understand this analogy try this demonstration, and watch what would happen: Put a halter with a lead rope attached to it on the horse and let the lead rope hang loosely to the ground. Think of this as the cable hanging from the end of the boom with a weight or load attached to it. As the boom of the crane rises, the load gets closer to the crane (the structure) and then the balance is compromised until where it is likely to flip backwards. You will see the same results in a horse. As the weight load draws into the body with a raised head, the balance is compromised forcing more weight and compression into the shoulders of the horse. This therefore will restrict the ability for the shoulders to work properly as the weight is forced toward the body. We have all heard the saying "where the head goes, the body follows".

(Relaxing the neck to lower the boom)

So if the **head and neck** are in a very upward posture due to contraction of the splenius muscle (think of a horse with a **ewe neck**) we not only see the effects on the hooves of the horse but also the muscle system that holds this posture. A raised head also creates more pressure into the lower portion of the neck (cervical) because as the head raises more weight is placed in the lower cervical area making it difficult for the horse to balance itself and even more difficult for it to support a rider. This will have a direct affect on the brachiocephalic (neck) muscles of the horse. The origin (anchor) is at the mastoid process just behind the jaw and the insertion (moving part) is at the point of shoulders. As this muscle contracts, it initiates the shoulder's movement cranially (toward the head) as well as assisting in lateral flexion from side to side. This will have a direct effect on the transmission because if the head is higher than normal, the shoulder is being pulled forward and this will create difficulty in the flexion of the limb. Almost as though your car has the brake on and you are stepping on the gas. You will not have efficient movement going forward.

(Beginning of Ewe neck)

This also creates a contraction of the long dorsal (back) muscle of the horse that originates in the lower cervical (neck) area and attaches in the pelvic area. This muscle's job is to contract creating the beginning of impulsion from the *rear*. Each side works almost simultaneously with each other yet independently. Here's another analogy for you to understand how this muscle works.

Locomotion analogy

Here's another analogy for you to understand how this simultaneous yet independent muscle action works. Think of a train in the old movies when it was leaving the station, the arm attached to the wheels on each side worked independently. They didn't push/pull in the same direction at the same time. One side pulled and then the other side pulled until the train was in full motion. As quickly as they moved they still moved opposite of each other.

This is the impulsion of a horse. Therefore, if the horse has a high head carriage and the back muscles are in a contracted state (as in a flat back horse) the impulsion is lessened. Try this experiment and tilt your head back by flexing your neck and then run forward. Not too easy is it? By the way, movement of the poll is also limited.

Looking at the poll visual & assessment

Does the horse have a tendency to hold its head up higher in one direction? An obvious sign would be to look at how/where the head carriage is. Is it left, straight or right? The muscles directly behind the horse's ears are the rectus capitis muscles, which are the muscles that lift the horse's head in a yes motion. To check this, place one hand gently behind the ears at the poll and the other with an open hand, palm upward, and gently but firmly hold the lower jaw just behind the chin. Now feel—and if you can—look at the size of the muscle on each side. You may also raise and lower the head in a yes motion each direction (left and right) to determine if there is more restriction on one side or more freedom of motion on the other—in other words symmetry.

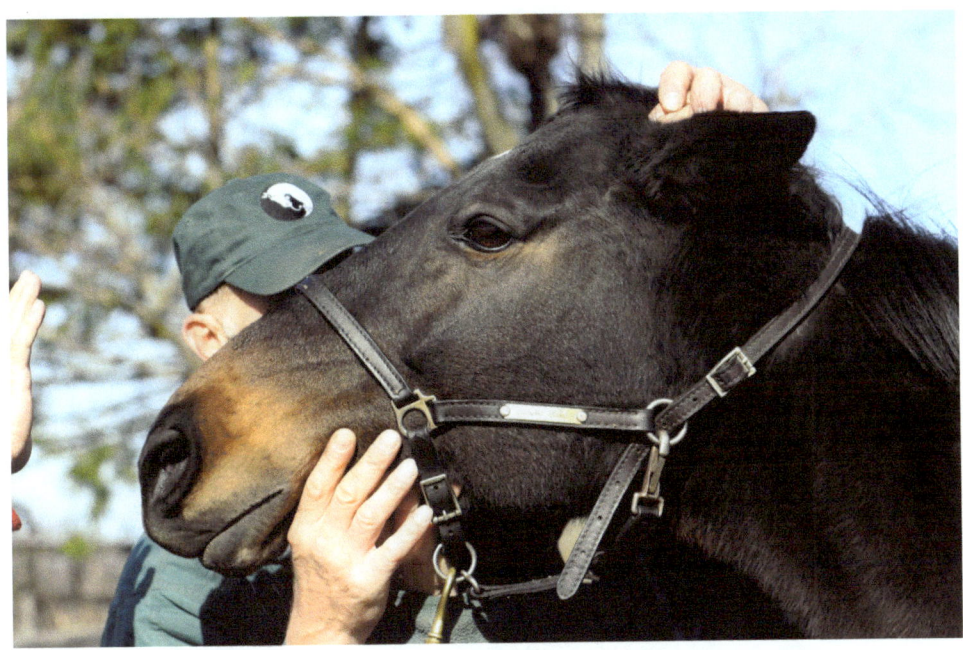

(Proper hand placement in assessing the poll)

(Checking poll from right side)

Looking at the chest visual assessment

Does the horse have the same or equal distance between the chest muscle and the leg? The tighter side of the chest will have created a flare of the hoof because the tension of the (transverse pectoral) muscle. This muscle draws the limb inward (adducting) causing more pressure to the outside of the hoof. This is because the center of the horse's weight falls in the center. So the closer the stance or base the horse has, the more pressure to the outside (lateral) portion of the hoof wall. The wider the stance is, the more pressure you have to the inside (medial portion) of the hoof wall. Try doing this . . . Extend your arms with closed hands (fists) and lean forward into a wall. Now bring one hand and arm closer to the other and you will see how you changed the pressure not only in your arm but also in your fist. More pressure to the inside pushes the blood flow to the outside. Pressure on the outside of your fist forces the blood flow to the inside.

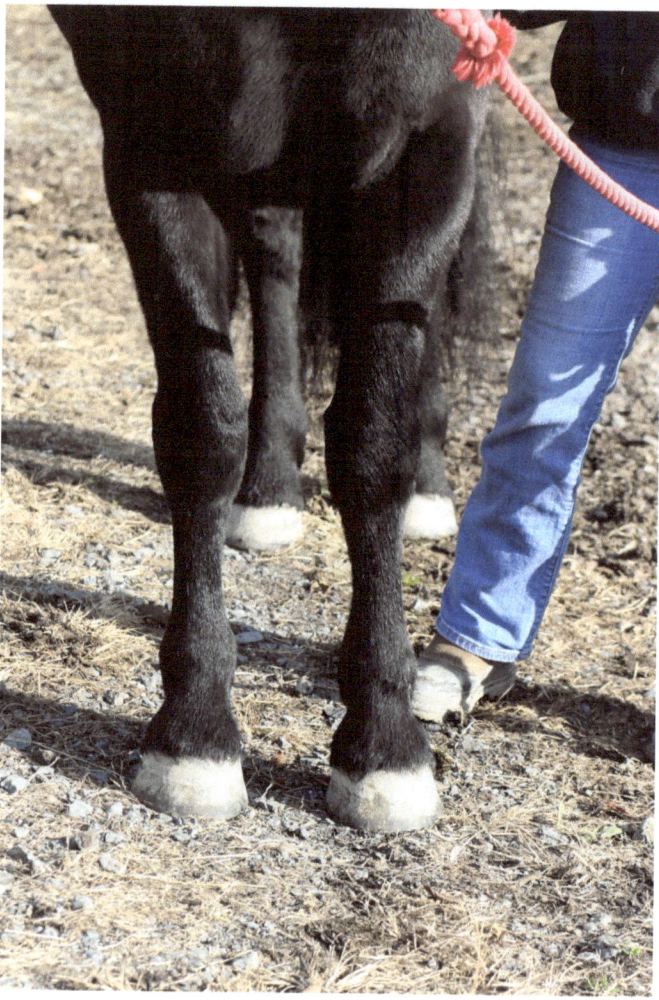

(Chest Muscles)

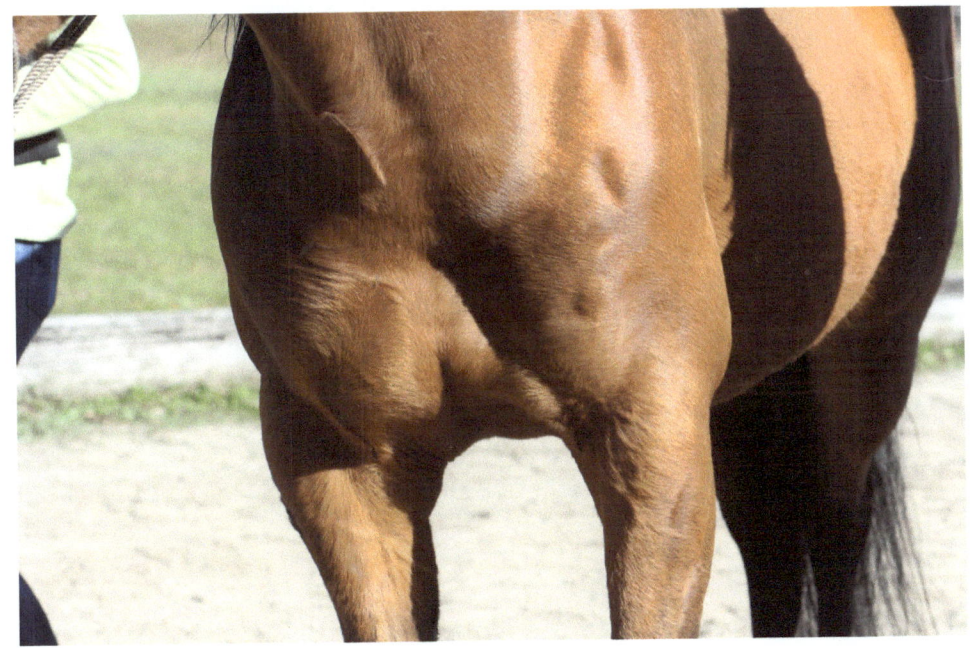

(Space of chest)

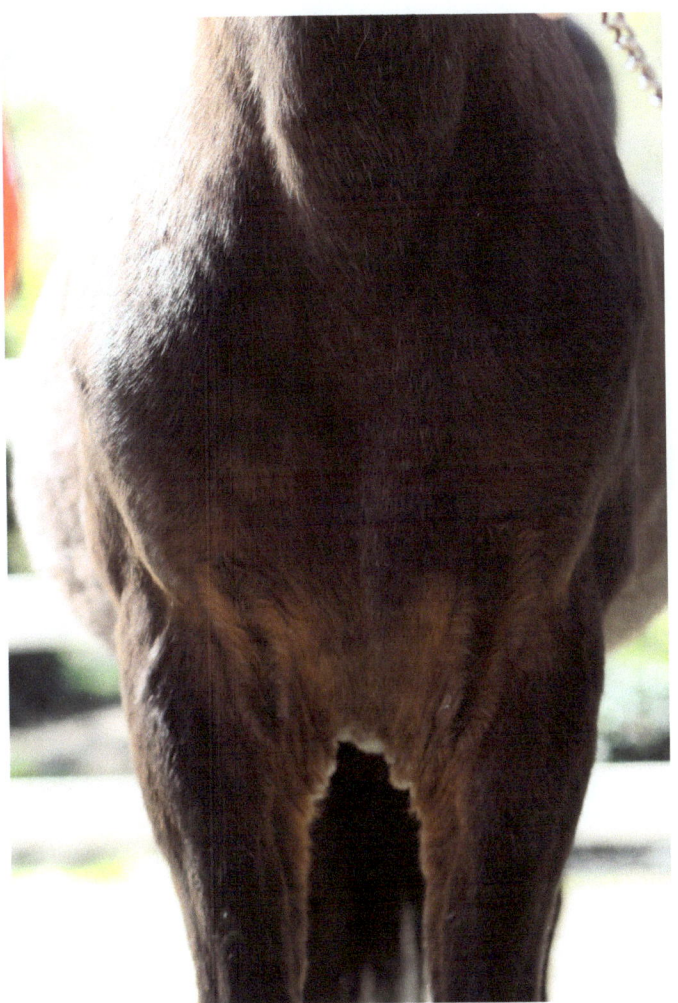

(Base narrow/Closed chest)

Looking at the shoulders visual/ assessment

When looking at the shoulders of your horse, you should stand on each side and do a comparison as to size and shape. Then stand directly behind the horse and look forward toward the head to assess the position and muscle mass of each side. You can also feel the position as well as the muscle mass to determine the balance of the shoulders. A horse with a lower heel on one side, more than likely, will have a more developed and posterior (backward) set of the shoulder.

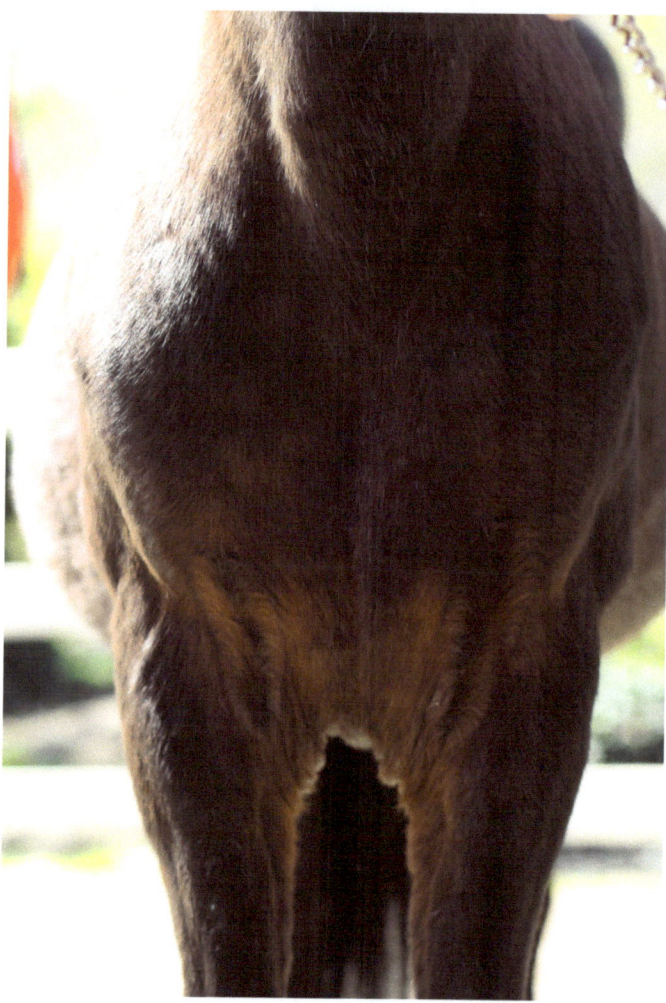

(Asymmetric Shoulders)

(Looking at top of scapula)

(checking muscle mass)

Looking at the thoracic Body visual assessment

Without getting too complicated here, I will refer to only one of the major muscles of the thorax: The serratus ventralis thoracic muscle. This is the muscle is seen on the underside of the horse, and it attaches the thoracic body (rib cage) to the shoulder. This muscle serves dual functions. When it contracts it expands the rib cage allowing for inspiration or the drawing of air into the lungs, and secondly when a horse shifts its weight to one side it is a supporting muscle. More tension on one side also leads to a larger foot on that side, due to weight shift and load combined with muscle & tendon tension. Now consider all the horses you may know that are sensitive to the girth. If this muscle is already tight and the horse is having difficulty getting a full breath, they will be sensitive and irritated because now it is even more difficult to get the air in and breathe. Think of the horses that make a blowing sound as they work.

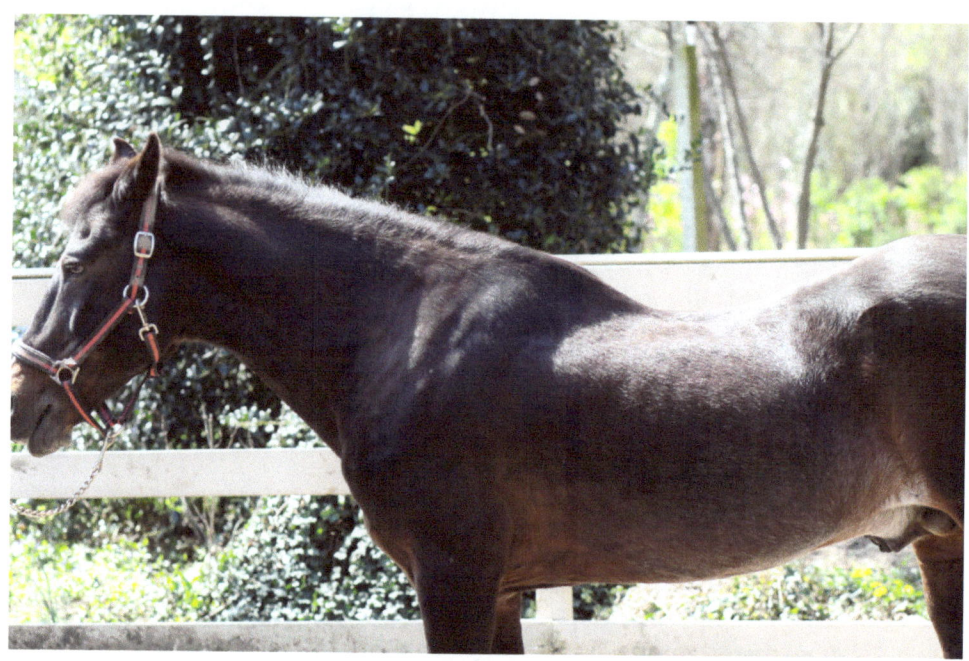

(Thoracic Body)

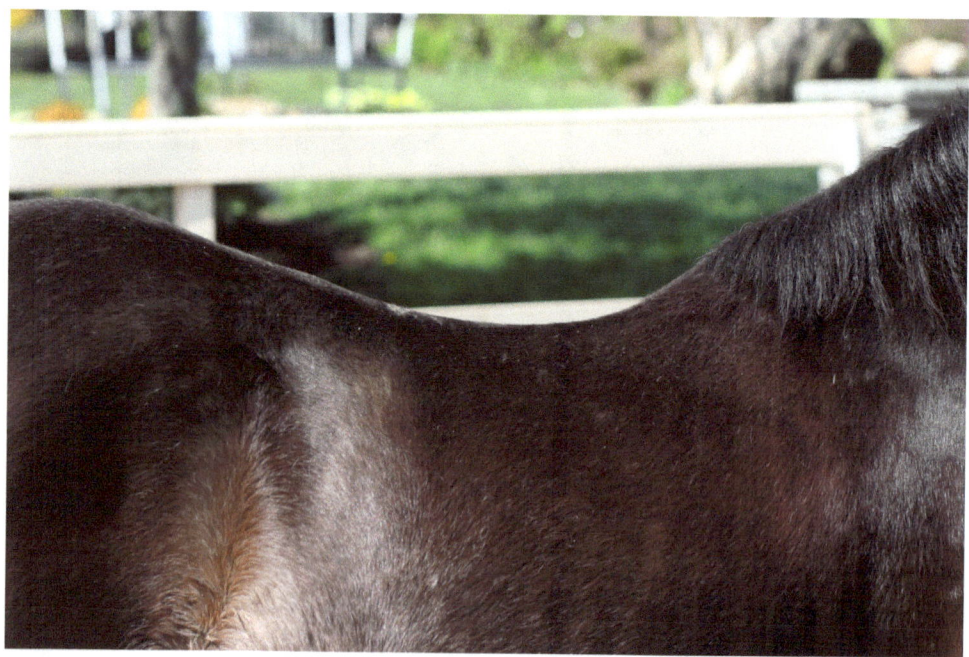

(Thoracic Body)

Looking at the Oblique muscles a visual assessment

The oblique muscles of the horse are the muscles that attach the thoracic body to the pelvis. In humans we call them "love handles". When you can see these muscles in the horse very prominently, you will see they generally have a fairly low tail set and the points of the hips (tuber coxae) will be obviously raised (pelvis tilted backwards). Since they are part of the abdominal muscle group, tension in these muscles will also restrict hind end impulsion. Try doing this . . . flex (tilt your pelvis forward) and walk at the same time. Not very comfortable walking is it? This is how the horse feels with tension in the abdominal muscles. You will notice by flexing your pelvis you are also tightening your abdominal muscles. This also causes you to round your lower back. Now if you had a tail, where would your tail set be?

(Oblique muscle)

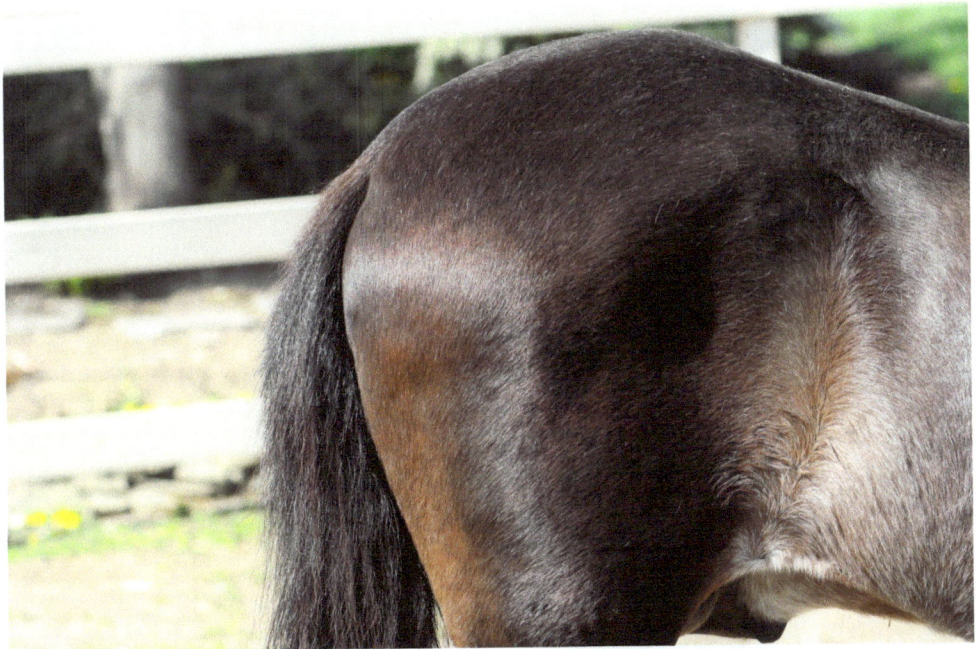

(Tension in oblique muscle: perfect for jaws of life)

Abdominal muscles visual assessment

As stated earlier under muscle function, it is a fact that every muscle has an opposing muscle. The abdominal muscles oppose the long back muscle. The function of the abdominal muscles is to draw the hind legs toward the body, and as stated above the back muscles initiate the pelvis and legs to move away (extend) from the body. The abdominal muscles oppose the long back muscle. Tension in the lower abdominal area will cause tension to the hip flexor muscles that flex the pelvis under the horse. Think of a horse that stands under from behind. Another thing to observe is the upward curvature of the abdomen.

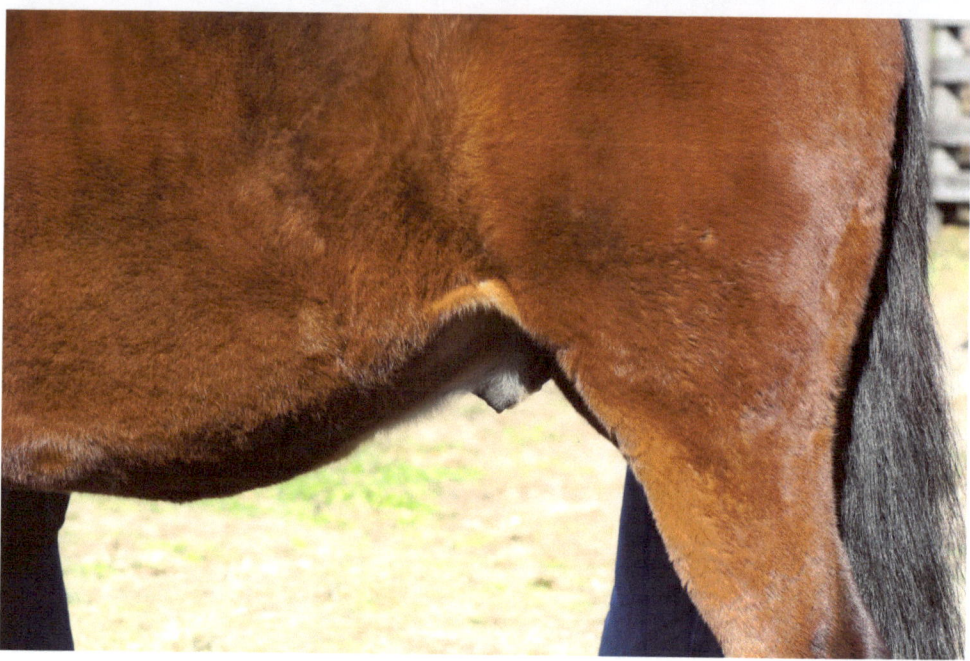

(Upward Curvature)

Try doing this . . . tighten your lower abdominal muscles and breathe at the same time. You will see that you can breathe, but it is fairly difficult. You will also feel that it is easier to exhale that to inhale. Now think of the horse you hear making a blowing noise as he works. He is forcing out the air with the hope of forcing the air in. They are experiencing the same thing you do when you tighten your lower abdomen . . . difficulty in breathing. To help them get more air into the body you can give your horse some peace. This will be discussed in the pages to follow.

The speed boat/anchor (the pelvis) analogy & visual assessment

Imagine this: 5 people are seated in a speedboat and the four passengers are all sitting in the rear or back of the boat. If the driver accelerates the boat with all the weight toward the rear of the boat, the front of the boat is going to rise due to the fact of gravity (weight) lowering the rear where the forward impulsion is being generated.

Let's look at it this way. If you view the pelvis (hips) of the horse as a speedboat and look at the tail as the anchor to the boat, and asked yourself "is the anchor **(tail)** up (high) or down (low)"? A horse with a low tail set is the horse that rises upward in its initial forward movement, whereas a horse with a level tail set or raised anchor will have its initial hind end impulsion pushing forward and not upward. If the tail set is too high you will observe a horse with a very flat back due to excessive tension of the long back muscle. This will also limit the impulsion from behind (remember locomotion) because the long back muscle is in a tense state, and since contraction of this muscle is what initiates forward impulsion from behind, if you have limited contraction you will have limited impulsion. Either one of the less than ideal postures of the horse we just discussed, will result in the same situation . . . limitation of impulsion from behind. Also, you can assess the position of the pelvis by looking at the tail as center and determine if one hip appears to be higher on one side. The higher hip is always the weight bearing leg.

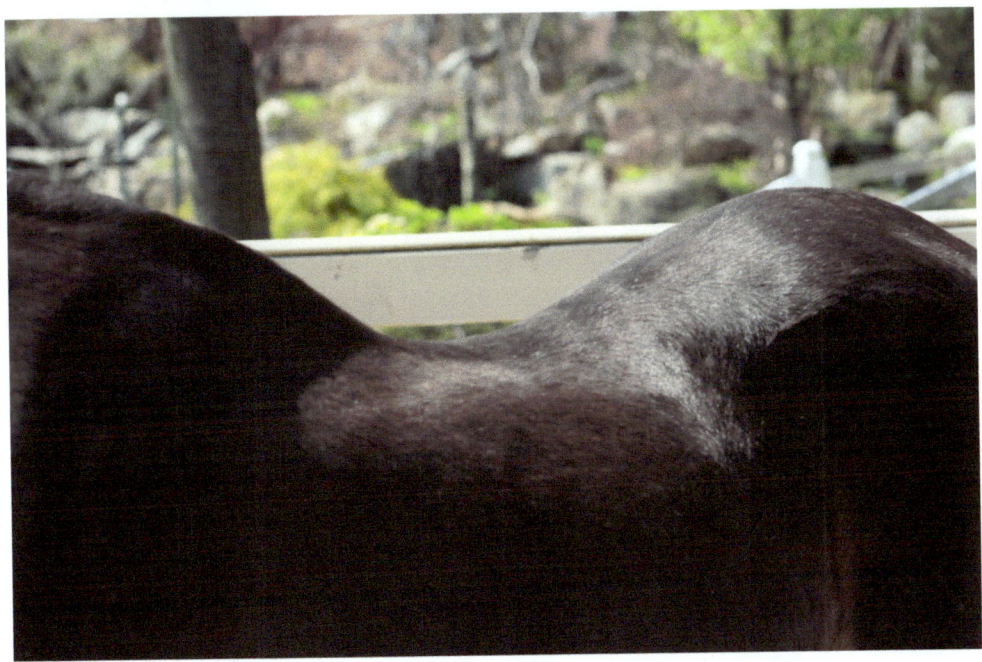

(Posterior pelvis)

Looking at the hind legs visual assessment

While standing behind the horse; look at the hind legs on both sides for equal muscle development. Also look at each side individually to determine muscle mass on both sides. We already discussed the horse with excessive tension in the abdomen. Again this is a horse that will be "standing under". A horse with excessive tension in the top line will be a horse that is "camped out". A "base narrow" horse as well as a "cow hocked" horse's will have excessive tension in the adductor muscles (gracilis/semitendinosis which are the muscles between the legs).

Hind Legs

Hind Legs

Stand and point your toes out and your heels in and you will feel the tension in between your legs. Now walk! A horse with a "base wide" stance has excessive tension in the abductors (quadriceps) on the outside of the legs. To feel this simply widen your legs . . . now walk in either of these postures and you will feel what the horse feels.

Fascial adhesions of the hock assessment

Many horses I see with hock problems stem from fascial adhesions of the hock. To understand this more easily, I ask you to slightly bend your arm at your side as if your arm is the back leg of the horse and your elbow is the point of hock (calcaneal bone). Now notice how easily you can move (pull) the skin from your elbow. You should be able to easily move the skin from the point of hock in the horse. Why is this so necessary? So it will bend easily. Suppose someone put saran wrap around your arms at the elbows and then asked you to do push—ups; you could likely perform this exercise, but with restriction and joint limitation.

To check for this you first **GENTLY** clasp your hand around the back of the hock and **GENTLY** pull away closing fingertips to palm. **Do not grab** too hard because if they are restricted, it will be uncomfortable. Think of peeling tape off yourself or a sticky band-aid. So Again . . . GO **Slow**.

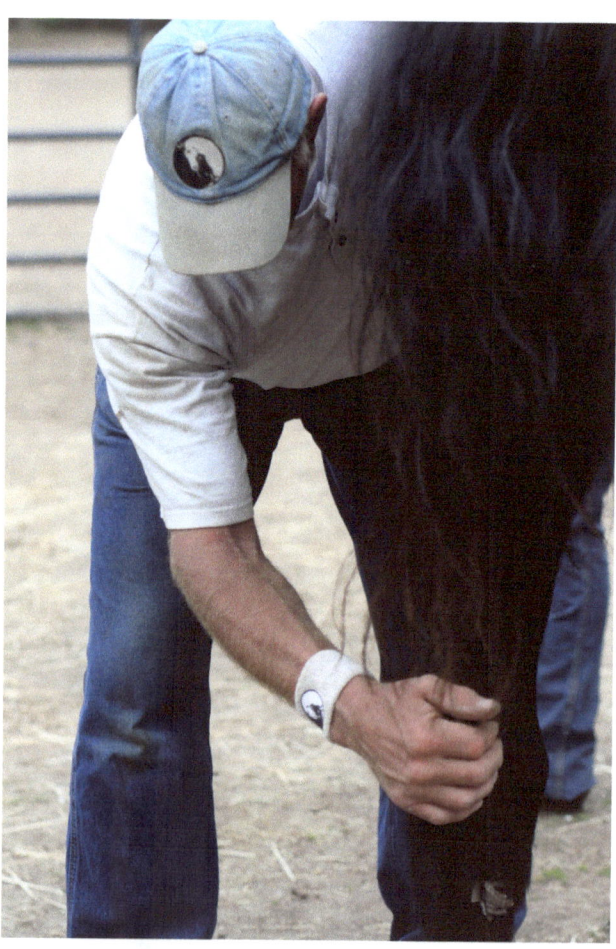

(Checking for fascial adhesions)

(Checking for fascial adhesions)

Chapter 4

TECHNIQUES

Now that you have learned to **look** for, and **see** imbalances, I will share with you a few easy to **understand**, and easy to apply techniques to improve your horse's posture and performance. When applying the reflex point techniques I would like you to think of doing them in sets and repetitions ***= sets and reps**

Start with 3 sets of 5 reps and increase your sets and reps as your horse strengthens. Your goal could be 5 sets of 8 reps.

Restoring balance in the poll technique *

While applying light to moderate pressure to the larger muscle (rectus capitis) gently raise and lower the head in a yes motion in the opposite direction of the larger side. (**NOTE: If the muscle on the right side is larger have the horse's head facing slightly to the left**.) This will loosen the larger muscle and stimulate the weaker one. It will also help to restore proper movement of the atlanto-occipital joint (where the head and neck connect).

(Restoring balance in the poll)

Water Ski analogy & technique

When you think of seeing someone water ski, you see them hold the rope and lean backwards. This is the same concept used in doing a tail pull for the horse. *Get* a firm grasp of the tail by wrapping the tail around your hand (**Important**) behind the last tail vertebrae and leaning backwards. **DO NOT PULL but LEAN** backward, making sure the tail is completely straight, to achieve the result you are looking for. This is used to help strengthen the back (top line). Most people believe they are stretching the horses back, but you are actually allowing them to stretch the lower abdomen and hip flexors. To prove this, do the exercise and have someone stand on the side of your horse and perform the suggested technique. You will see the abdomen relax and when you let go they will see the abdomen tighten. **So please do not pull without gently releasing the pressure**. Also as the horse pulls against you, he will be transferring his weight more to the front of their feet that is a great exercise for horses with low heels. By loading toward the toe and raising the heel they are getting more blood flow to a part of the hoof that is obviously lacking. **This should be a consistent pull, which you may hold for about 30 seconds at a time. ***

(Finding last tail vertebrae for tail wrap)

(Proper tail wrap for waterskiing)

Going to the gas station analogy & technique*

Muscles are fueled by oxygenated blood. Blood flow to a muscle is determined by the state a muscle is in, be it contracted or relaxed. When you contract a muscle or muscle group, its opposing muscles relax and stretch (lengthen). As the muscle contracts you create vasoconstriction or constriction of the capillary walls that carry the blood to the fibers. To oxygenate the muscles quickly you can do compressions on the muscle. Think of doing CPR. You are pressing downward with moderate pressure with a relaxed open palm and releasing, in a series of pumps (**compress each placement 5 times**). By doing this you are pumping oxygenated blood into the muscle tissue as well as nutrients carried by the blood. This technique should be used before you try to ask for the elongated muscle/group to contract. Just like going to the gas station to fill your tank before you take a road trip, you want to have fuel to get where you want to go. The same concept applies to the muscles. If the muscles you are stimulating are going to be more active by your intention of using a reflex to stimulate it, they need the fuel to work. A muscle that has been in an elongated or stretched state due to a passive or mild contraction of its opposite muscle has been deprived of oxygenated blood. If you stretch a rubber hose the passage way narrows. Think of muscle fibers as little rubber hoses, and as the opposing muscle lengthens it narrows the passage of blood. With a lack of proper blood flow the body is forced to use an alternate source of fuel. And that fuel consists of sugars. When the body uses this alternate source, it creates lactic acid, which creates muscle soreness.

(Proper hand position to perform CPR)

(Using an Octassager for compression)

Understanding Reflex Points technique *

A reflex point is a point on the horse that creates a specific movement. By stimulating it you are asking a specific muscle/group to contract through intentional touch. In doing this you are facilitating the opposite muscle to relax. Since muscles oppose each, other it is not possible to contract both sides at the same time. It also should be understood that you are actually strengthening both side at the same time. You are achieving this because you are relaxing the contracted muscle and contracting the elongated muscle hence restoring muscle balance.

Giving the horse peace analogy & technique using reflex points

When I describe giving the horse peace, it's in regards to two things. First, is your hand placement and configuration correct; secondly you must always be mindful that the purpose of this technique is to increase the ability for your horse to take a full breath of air.

You can give your horse peace by making the "peace sign" with your fingers. You will **gently** place your middle finger behind the 18th (last) rib and your index finger will fall between the 17th and 18th rib space. **Note**: If you are standing on the right side of the horse you will use you right hand. And if you are on the left, then you will use your left hand. Your thumb should then make contact with the oblique muscle (the external muscle that attaches the thoracic body to the pelvis). You will **gently** press inward and then **gently** upward. The responses you are looking for is for the abdomen to relax and lower, that side hind leg to relax and even extend (move backward away from the body) and you should physically feel and see the horse taking deeper breaths. **This is a constant hold and not performed in sets or reps. Important . . . . remember to breathe!**

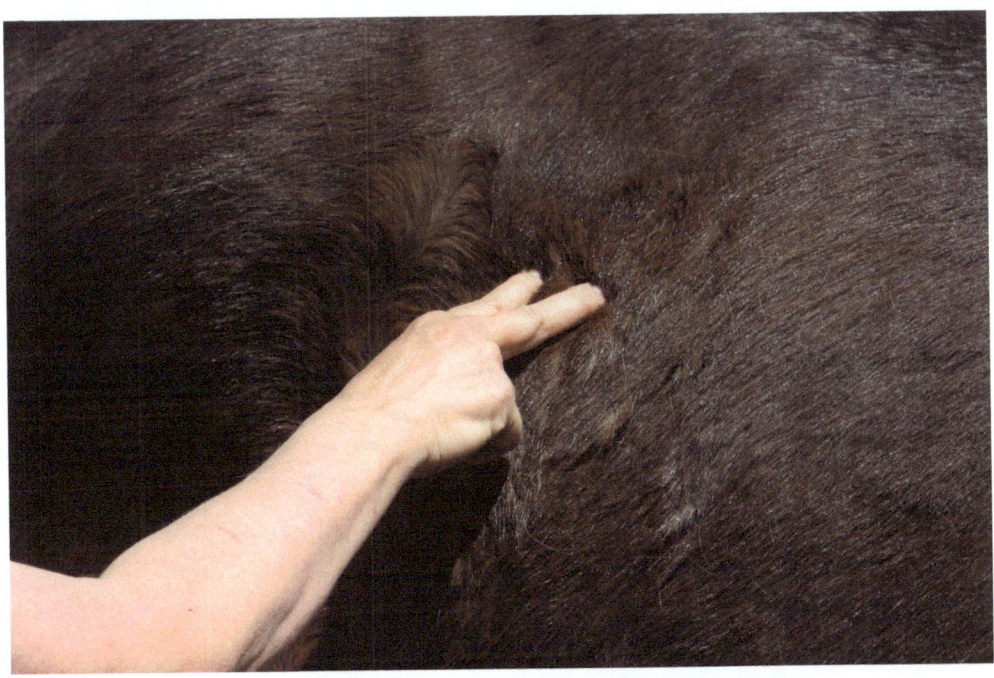

(Finger behind 18th rib / finger between 17th & 18th rib)

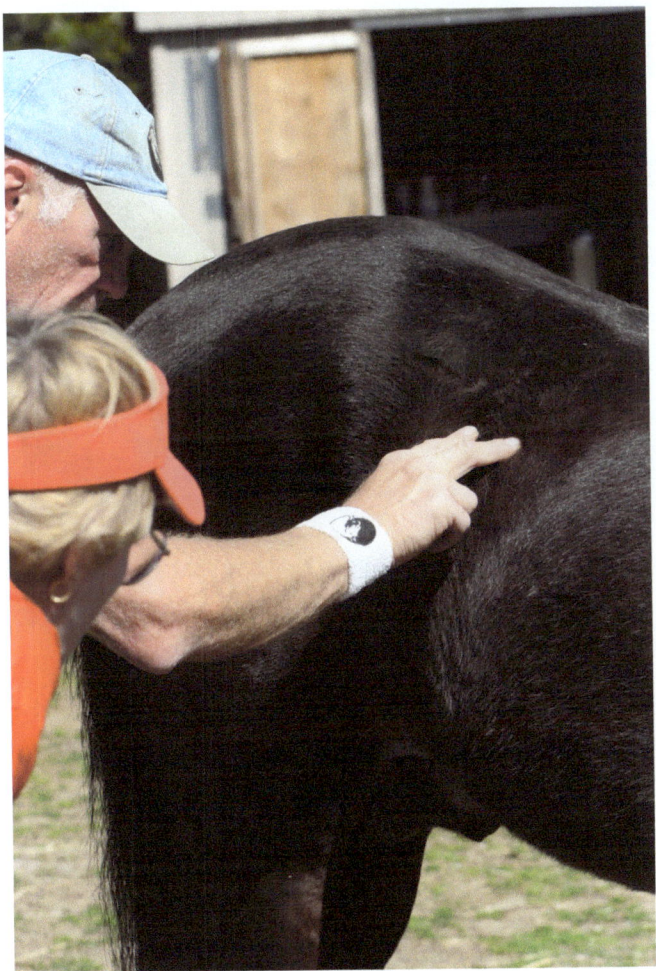

(Gently press inward and upward)

Jaws of Life analogy & technique using reflex point

The next technique described is what I call the "jaws of life". When you think of the "jaws of life" you think of the tool used to pry something open to save a life. This technique is used to relax the oblique muscles. If standing on the left side of the horse you will place the "blade" of your right hand (think karate chop) gently but firmly against the last rib and cross your left arm over the right and place your palm against the point of hip. Your greater pressure is in the direction of the pelvis (do not press hard in the direction of the ribs). To perform this correctly you will be facing the horse and apply your hands as described and then turn your body from above the waist toward the pelvis with moderate pressure driving off of your opposing leg. If standing on the right side of the horse you should have your right hand against the pelvic bone and cross your left arm over the right with light pressure against the 18th or last rib. The reaction should be the horse pushing back into your hand against their hip. This is also a back strengthening exercise because the horse is using the back muscles to assist in pushing forward which relaxes the oblique and abdominal muscles. **This is a constant hold and not performed in sets and reps.**

(Point of hip in palm of hand pushing away with this hand and blade of hand behind ribs)

Balancing the shoulders technique using reflex points*

To help balance the shoulders, let's start with the more developed shoulder. Remember that horses will move into your pressure. You will stand in front of the horse's shoulder and place an open hand facing the rear of the horse with your thumb pressed against the lower point of shoulder. Press directly inward on the point of shoulder and the horse should lean into your pressure, causing it to load toward the toe and rotate the shoulder forward. For the shoulder that is less developed you will stand behind the horse on the opposite side of that shoulder and press directly toward that opposite shoulder. This will ask the horse to lean backward into your pressure by loading the front leg and pushing against (or back into) you. You will observe the (trapezius) shoulder muscle get larger as the shoulder rotates backward toward you. **This is also great for the clubfoot horse.**

(Pressure towards opposite shoulder: Note opposite shoulder)

(Proper hand placement pressing towards opposite shoulder)

The Cranial and Caudal reflex points of the pelvis techniques using reflex points*

Use the cranial reflex to strengthen the top line and relax the abdomen. The caudal reflex point would strengthen the abdomen and stretch the top line. You can perform these reflex points to help your horse strengthen the weak muscles while stretching the muscles holding tension. Apply this technique with reps and sets in mind. Just as you would do in your work out, **repetition gets results.**

This technique is used for the horse that is "standing under" *

The location of the **cranial reflex point of the pelvis** is the reflex point closer to the head of the horse. If you draw an imaginary line from the points of the pelvis toward the spine, and press directly downward in the middle of your line with moderate pressure, you will see the long back muscle of the horse contract extending the pelvis. This should not require much pressure.

This technique is used for the horse that is "camped out" *

(Cranial reflex point of the pelvis to relax abdomen and extend the pelvis)

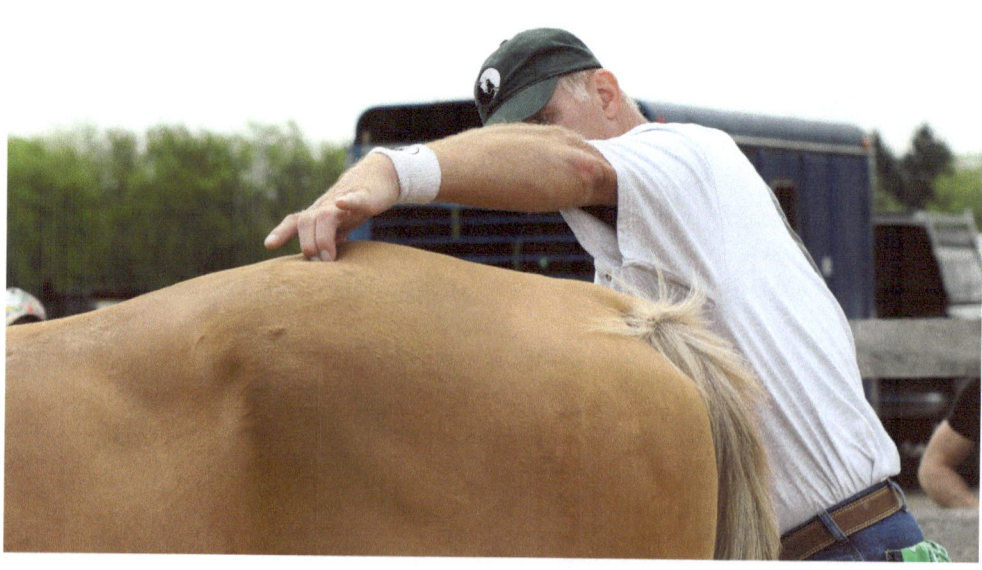

(By pressing these cranial reflex points you will see the tail "anchor" rise)

The **caudal reflex point of the pelvis** is the reflex point closer to the tail of the horse. If you stand behind the horse and lightly scratch or press on the ischium (bony prominence on each side of the tail) you will observe your horse tighten the abdominal muscles and lift its back (like a cat arching its back). This exercise will strengthen the abdominal muscles. The function of the lower abdominal muscles is to draw the hind limbs toward the body.

(By pressing the caudal reflex point, you will engage the abdomen and raise the back.)

Pulling the tail to the side technique for the "base narrow/cow hocked" horse*

This exercise will help strengthen the quadriceps muscles of the horse (outer leg). It is applied by standing directly on the side of the horse with its tail at a level position (not too high or too low) and pulling towards you. You will see the quadriceps contract, which forces the inner thigh muscles (adductors) to relax.

Releasing fascial adhesions in the hocks technique

As described previously, you should free the skin around the hock by gently but firmly grasping the skin between your fingertips and your palm and squeeze the skin away from the point of hock. You may also use just your fingertips and press them together from each side toward the back (point) of the hock. Then ask for the horse to lift his leg slightly so they can feel the freedom of movement.

Using these techniques is guaranteed to help your horse achieve and maintain better posture while restoring balance to the body.

Please go to my website for more information:

www.dinosbest.info

Acknowledgements

My Mother, God rest her soul

For all the love and encouragement you had given me as I grew from a boy to a man. You are forever in my heart.

And To My Father

Thank you for your guidance throughout my life, instilling a strong work ethic in me and teaching me to be a good man.

My accomplishments would not have been possible without you both and I am proud to say I am your son.

Edna Dixon

In 1980, at the transitional period in my life when I decided I wanted to help people by learning massage, I met Edna and little did I know how she would change my life. I remember our first meeting, and asking her with a big smile "so . . . . will you teach me massage?" . . . and her laughing and saying "no, I am going to teach you how to fix people". She would always say to me . . ."close your eyes and open your mind", words I will never forget. For sharing your knowledge and your guidance and training, I will always be grateful.

Joe Sansolo, DC

I thank you for also taking me under your wing as a friend and mentor and sharing your knowledge and expertise in the art of joint mobilization.

Sifu Bill Portrey

My martial arts instructor who shared his knowledge of an art that I have learned to incorporate into the work I perform. Understanding leverage without force has made a huge impact in the ability to mobilize the soft tissue and joints of a horse with ease.

Pat Whalen-Shaw equine massage instructor

Thank you for my initial instruction in the world of equine therapy, which allowed me to transition from human to equine therapy.

Spencer LaFlure, Horse Dentist and Mike Fragale, EQD (Equine dentist)

I am forever grateful to you both for the numerous hours of sharing your knowledge of equine dental pathology and the necessity of a balanced mouth.

Vernon Purdt and Randy DeBord Farriers

My thanks to you both for all the time spent together learning from, and working with each of you side by side, to enhance the results of our work and improve the lives of horses.

Randy, a special thanks to you for sharing your philosophy and your words of which I too now live by which is **"treat the horse with justice".**

Mary Ellen Hill-Pierce

Thank you for all you have done to help make this possible. You not only have hosted clinics, but attended others taking notes for participants and all of the great photos, which made this dream a reality. You truly are a voice for the horse.

Kelly Burke and Lisa Rodman

Thank you for assisting me in the editing of the manuscript.

To all my clients who have allowed me the opportunity to work with their horse and the experiences and learning that has come from it.

Dino previously worked on people for 17 years, specializing in muscular/skeletal dysfunction. During this time he worked with Chiropractors and Orthopedic Surgeons aiding in their patient's recoveries. He has also had a special attraction and love of horses so it only seemed natural for him to apply his expertise and knowledge to help horses. He started working on horses in 1996 after he received his certification in Equine Massage Therapy from the Optissage in Circleville, Ohio. His endeavor started slowly, but with lots of love, persistence and trust by the trainers, he was soon being referred to everyone on the show circuit.

Dino is privileged to say that his equine clientele has a range from back yard buddies to World Cup and Olympic level competitors. To watch Dino work with the horses is a sight to behold. His calming demeanor and respect for the horse enable him to get incredible results from his bodywork. He has had many veterinarians seek his expertise in evaluating injuries.

His methods are based on the simple basics of massage and stretching. He uses simple hand placements and body mechanics to ensure safety for both himself and the horse at all times. He listens to the horses and watches their reactions to determine the points that need the most attention. The horse's reactions to him are incredible.